# Maze Puzzle Book for

W9-CKE-470

This book belongs to:

_____

This book is filled with 101 amazing maze puzzles for hours of fun! Puzzles are separated into 3 levels, ranging from easy to challenging. All the solutions are at the end of the book.

This book features:
- 101 AMAZING MAZES
- CUTE IMAGES TO COLOR
- LARGE SIZE PAGES
- SOLUTIONS AT THE END
- PROGRESSING DIFFICULTY LEVELS
- COMPLETION CERTIFICATE AT THE END

## For the Parent

Mazes and activities involve hand eye coordination and help improve your kids dexterity and muscle memory through the constant practice of drawing a line through various obstacles. Doing maze activities also helps in nurturing the development of your child's brain, thought processes, problem solving skills, IQ and intelligence by having your child map out the best path to reach the goal in every activity.

# Level 1 - Simple Mazes

Let's start with some simple mazes.

Ready? Great - Let's go!

# PLAYTIME

# HI TURTLE

# BIKING

# PLAYGROUND

# FIREMAN

# MR. TURTLE

# HUNGRY DOG

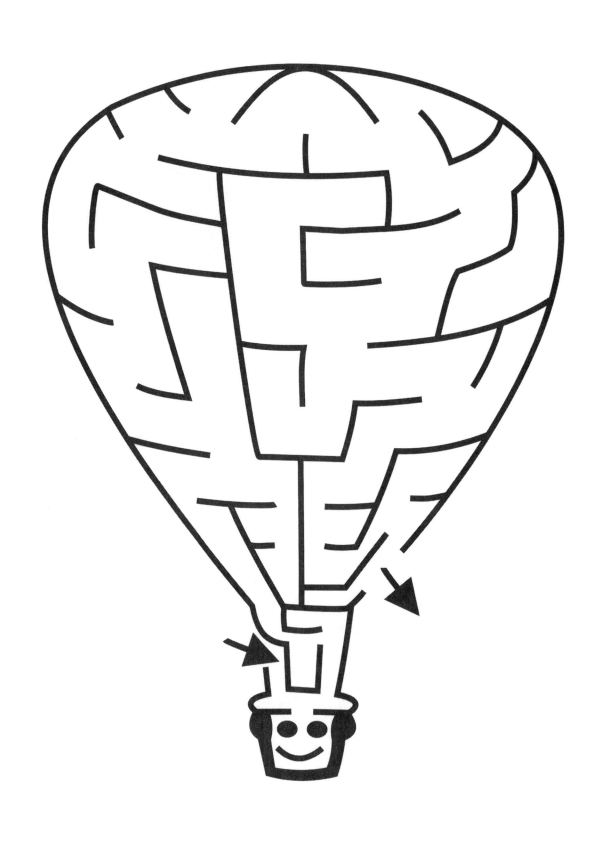

# UMBRELLA

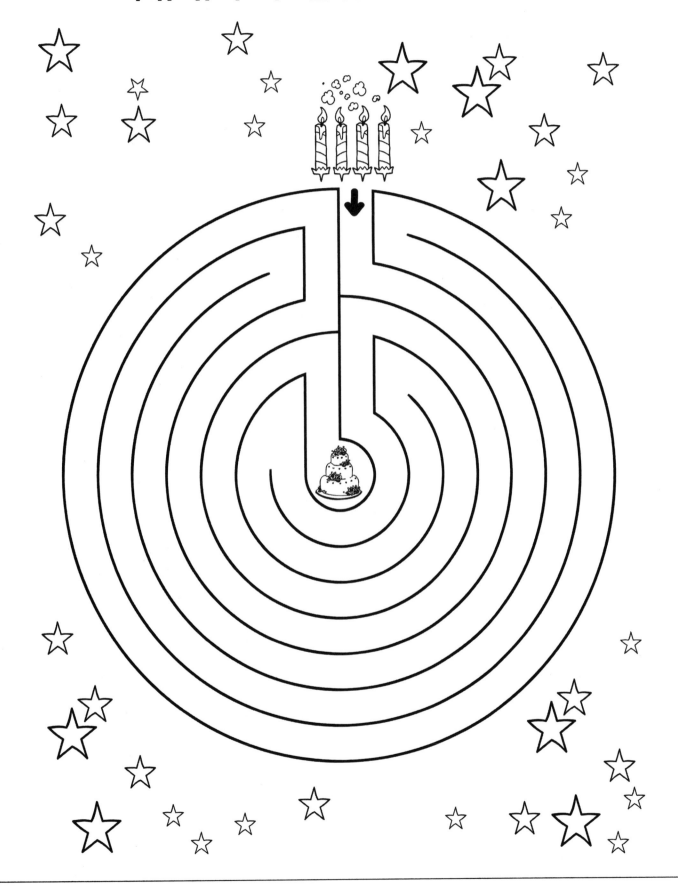

# EASTER

# TISSUE BOX

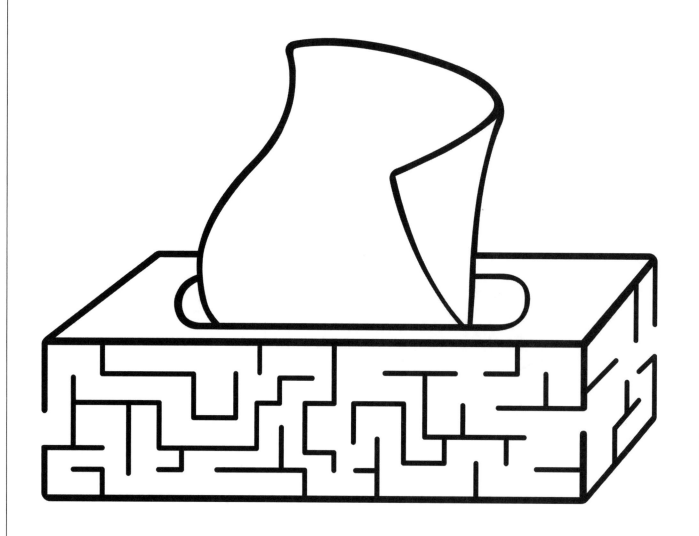

# ELEPHANT

# LADYBUG

# RABBIT

# UNLOCK

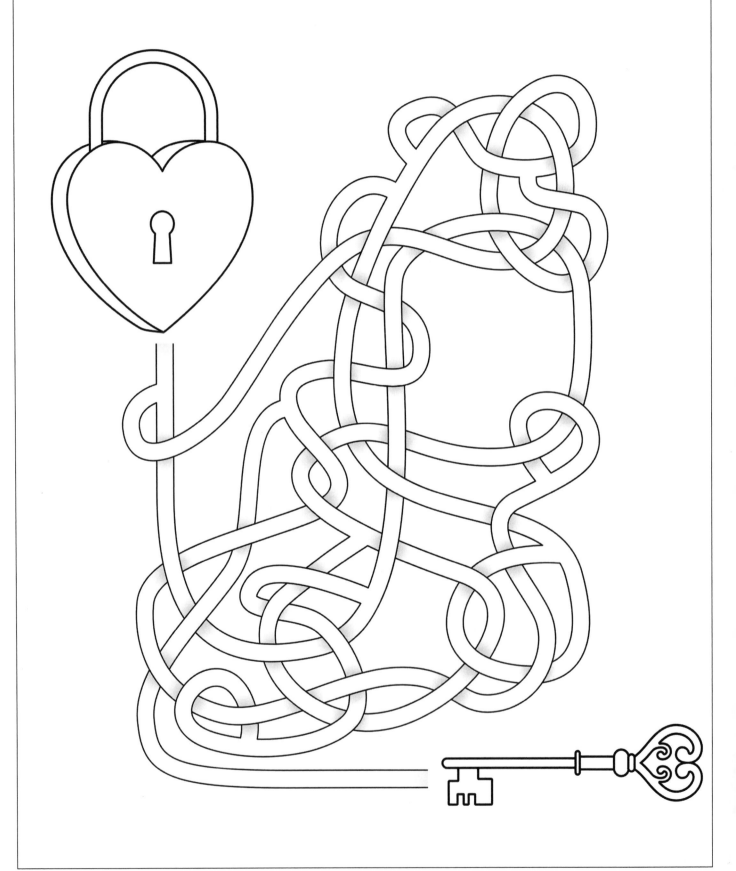

LOST AND FOUND

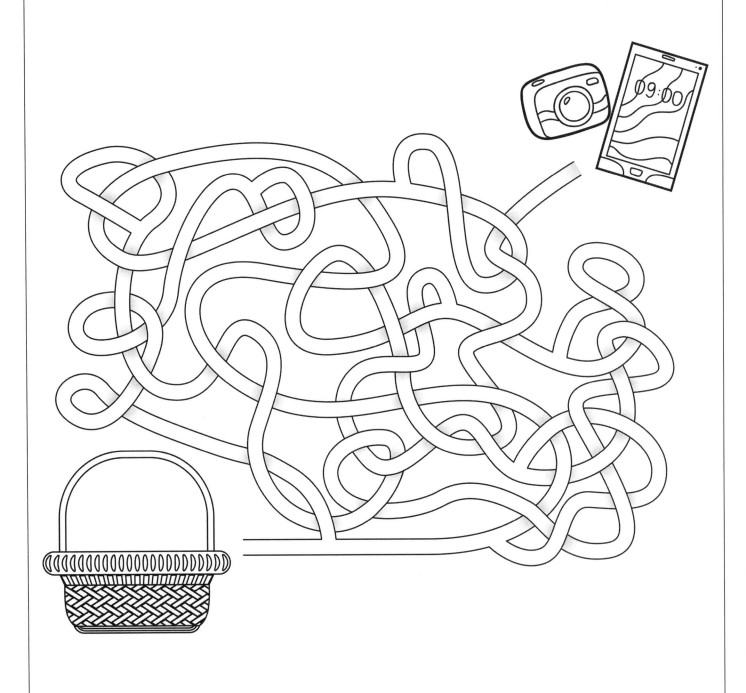

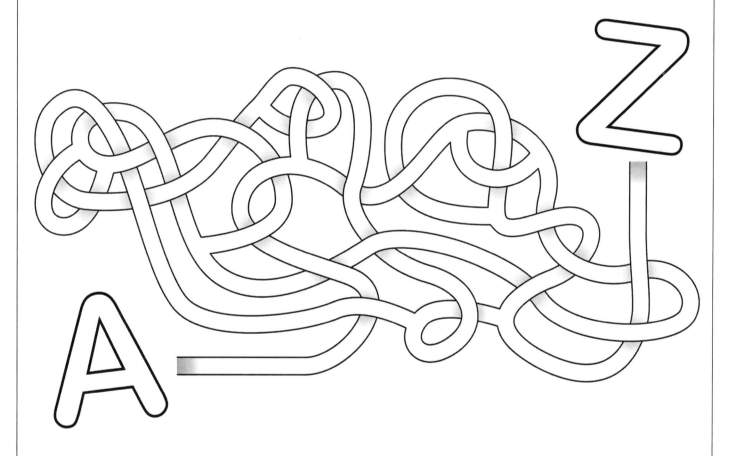

# 30  WATER THE FLOWER

# BASKETBALL

# SAFARI

# CATERPILLAR

# Level 2 - More Advanced Mazes

Great job - You are amazing!

Let's continue and solve some more advanced mazes.

# AVOCADO

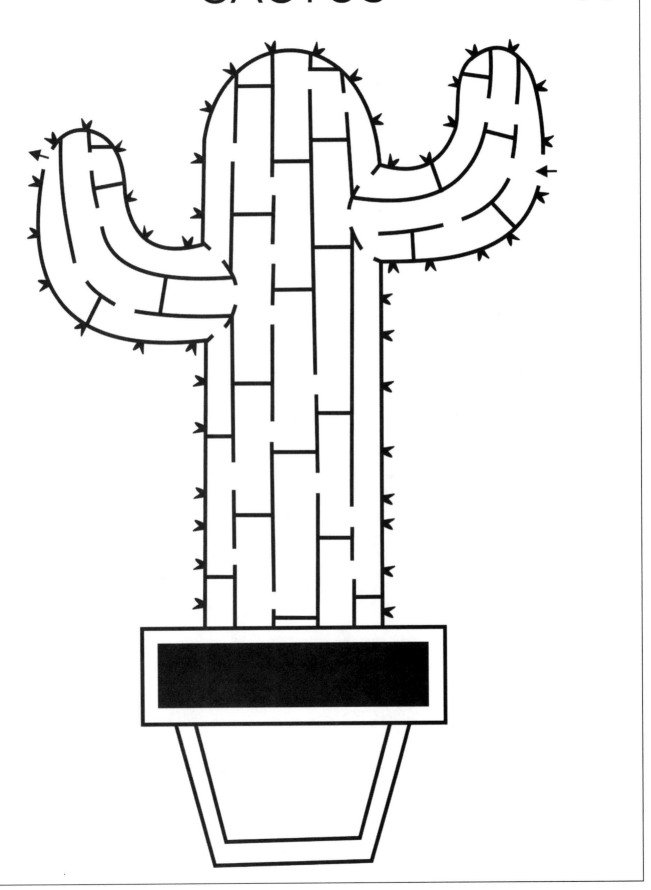

MERMAID

# BEE

HELLO SNOWMAN

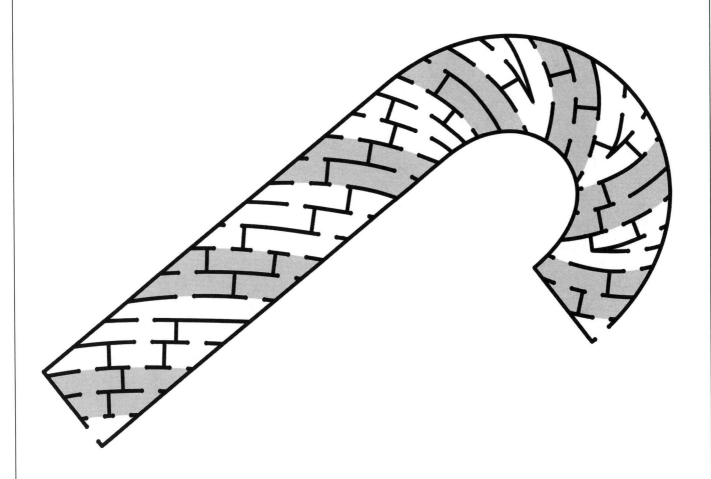

# MR. WHALE

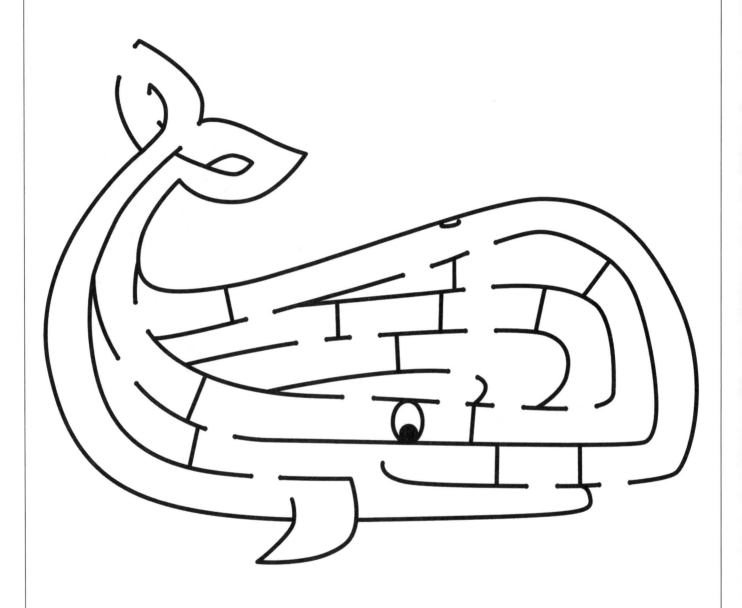

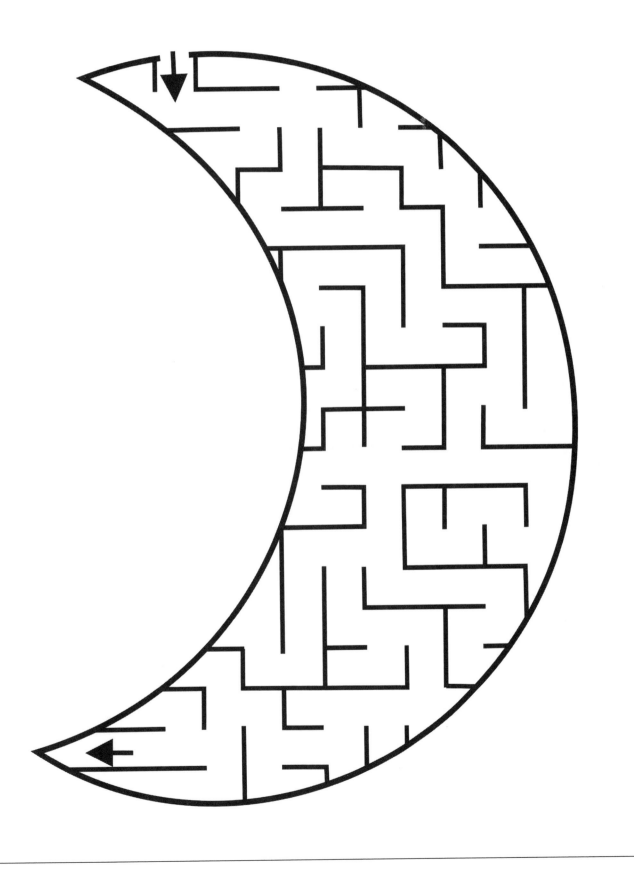

# HAPPY DOG

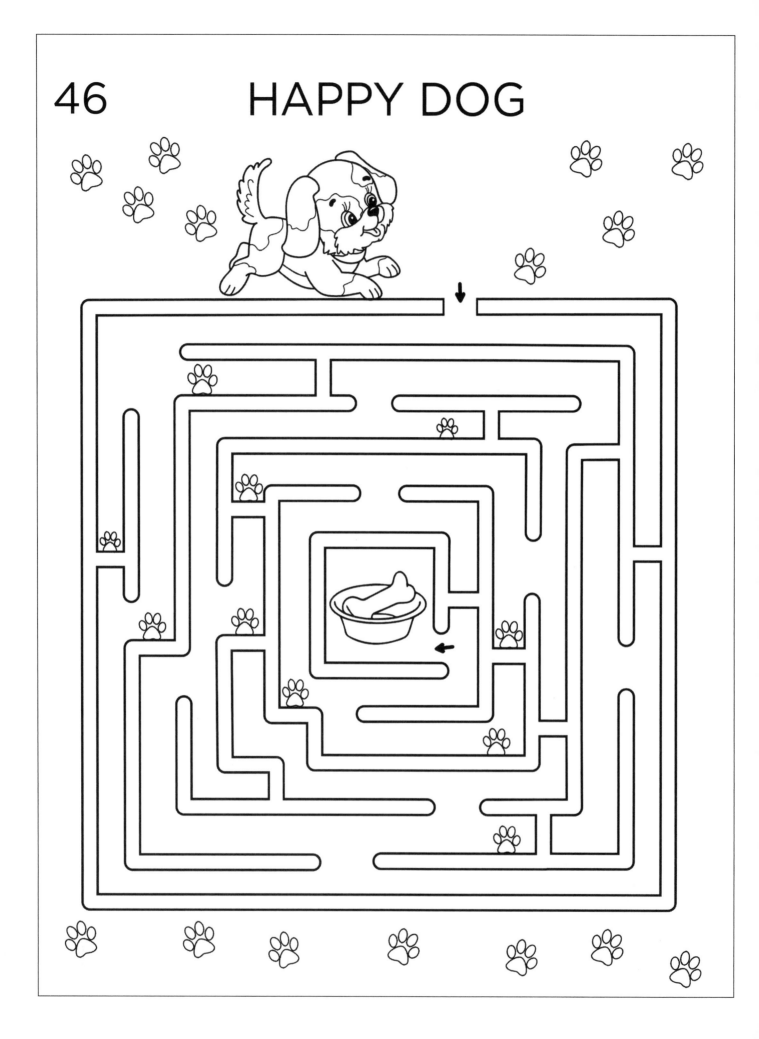

# HI SNAIL

# ROCKET SHIP

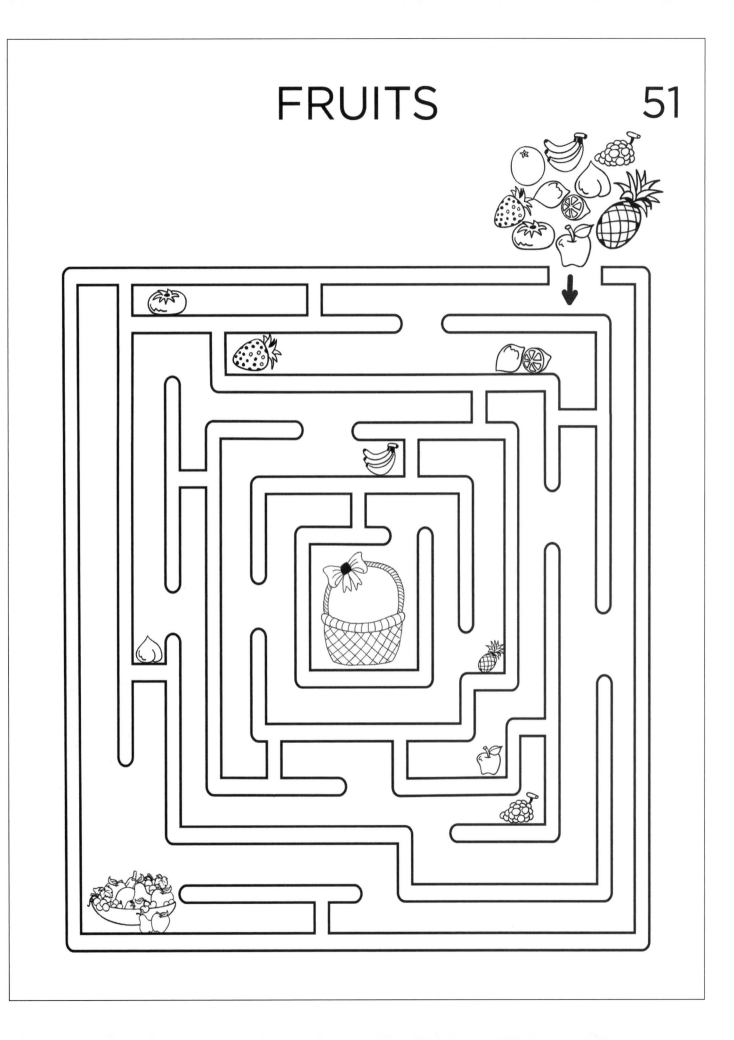

# TRUCK

## 54 LOST CHICKEN

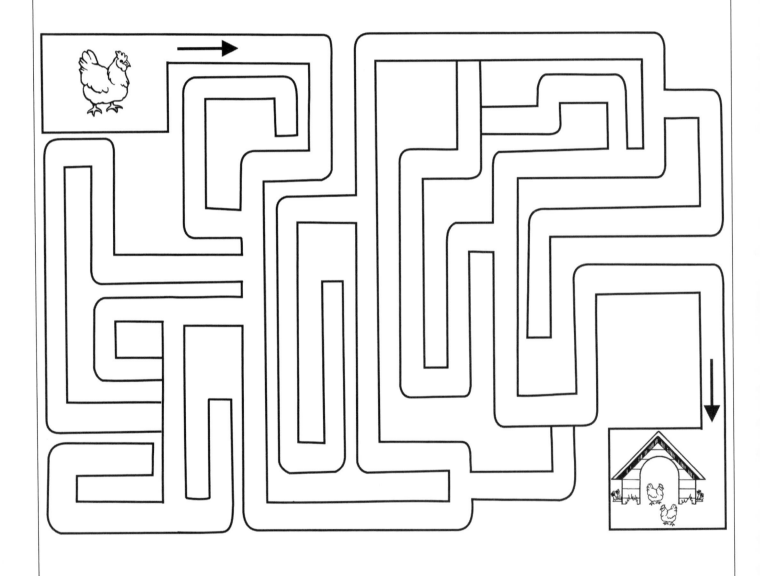

# 56 GROCERY SHOPPING

# DOCTOR

# BUSINESS

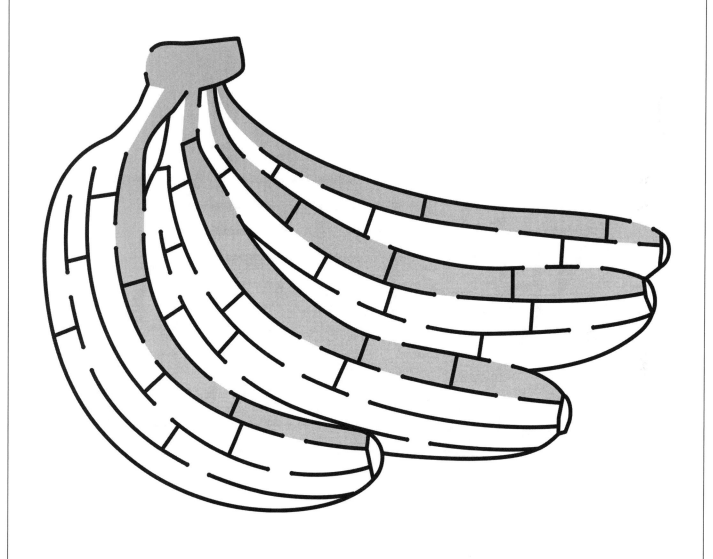

# BUS TRIP

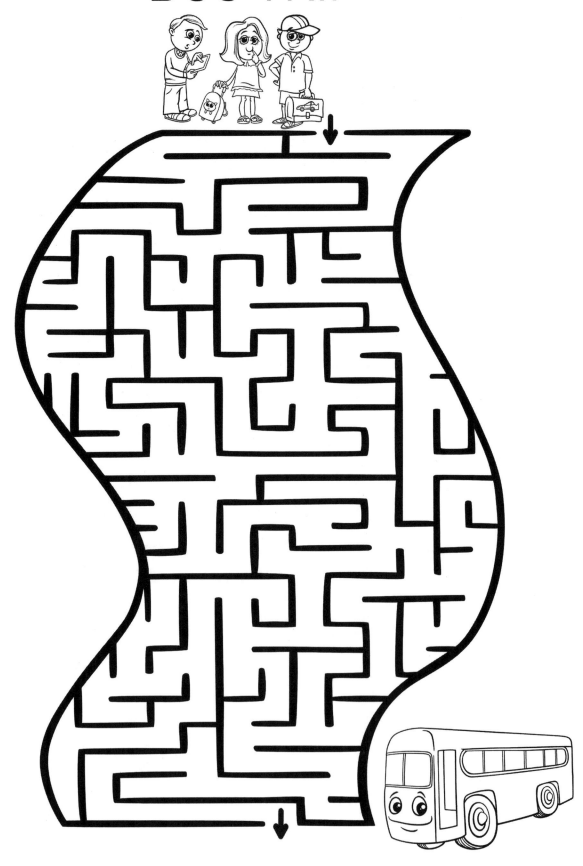

# GUITAR

# CHRISTMAS

# Level 3 - Complex Mazes

Well done! You are really great at this.

This is the last level with the most complicated mazes. Let's see if you can also solve them.
I know you can do it!

# DAILY CHORES

# SHELTER

# 76 DINING TABLE

# COMING HOME

# MS. GIRAFFE

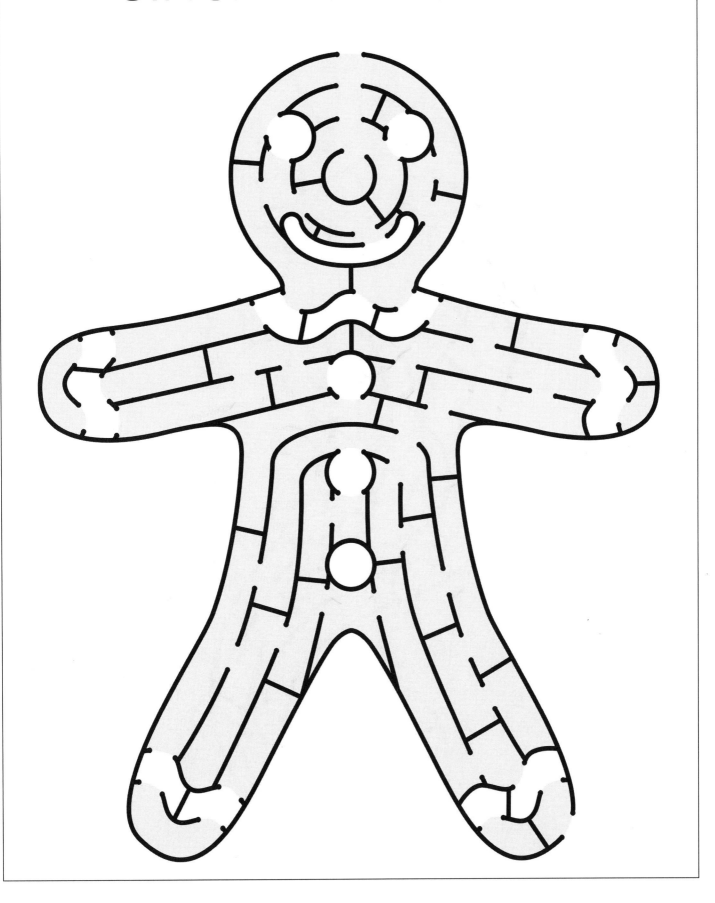

# SEAHORSE

# PINEAPPLE

SUNDAY THREAT

# HELICOPTER

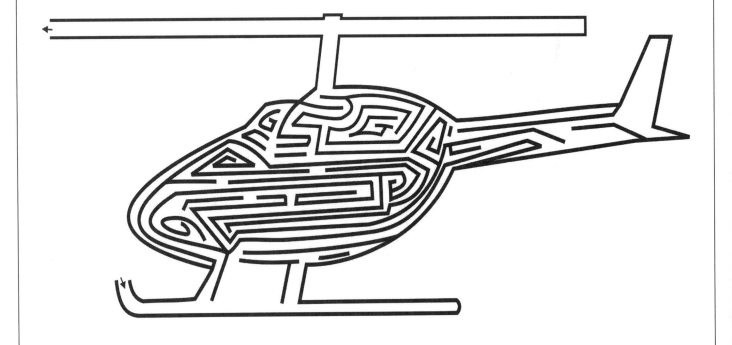

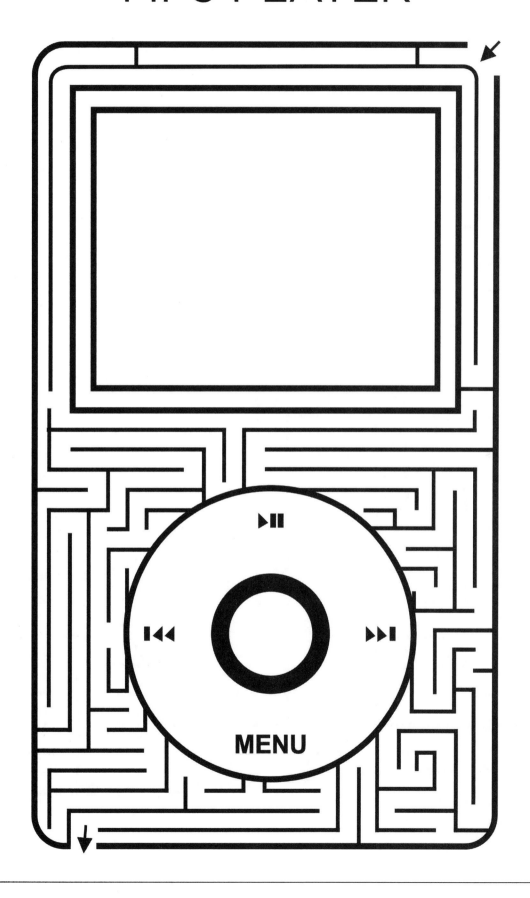

RAIN BOOTS

# SPIDER WEB

91

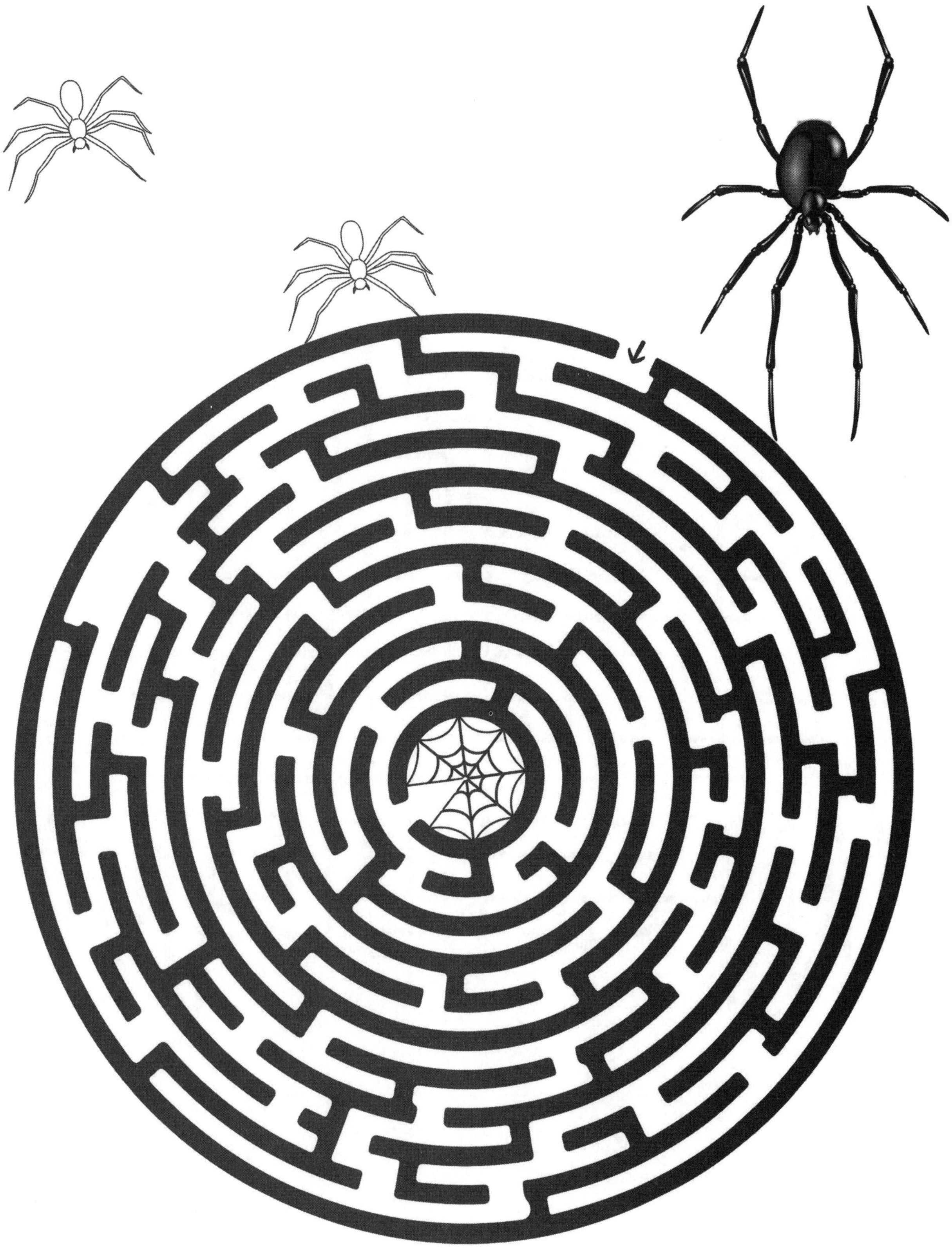

# MR. CRAB

# WAY HOME

# BALL

THANKSGIVING

# FLOWER

# BALLOONS

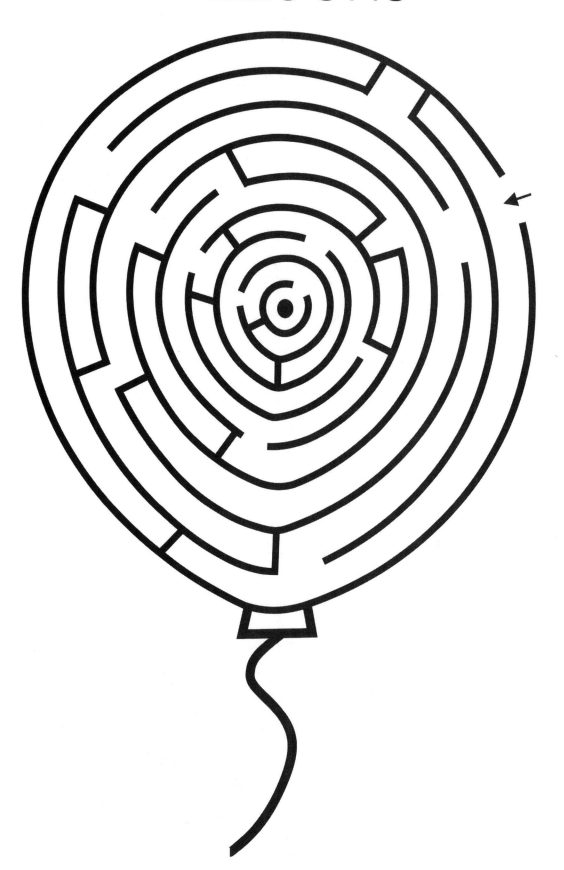

# TUCAN



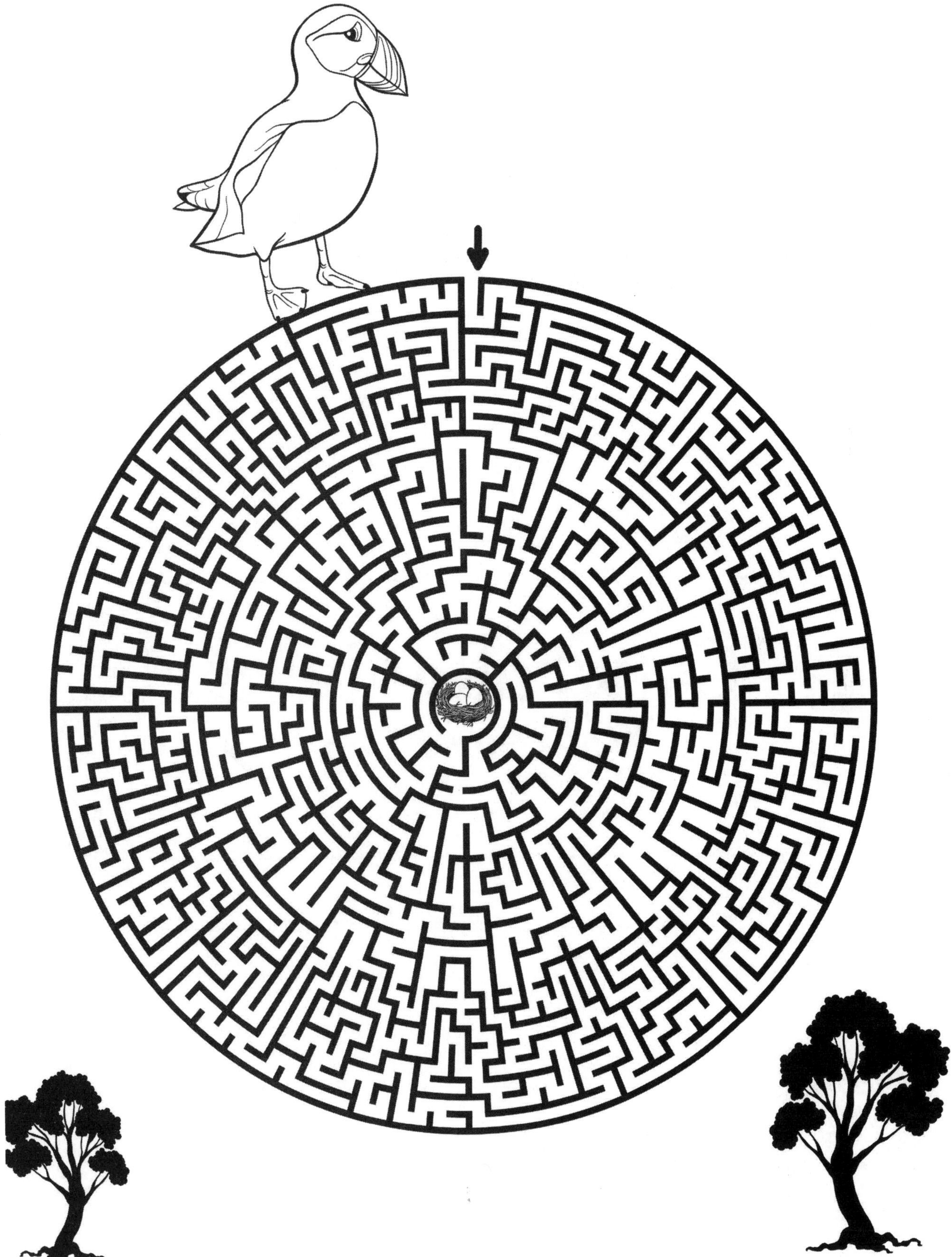

# CONGRATULATIONS!

Great job. You rock! If you want to continue with some more mazes, just send me an email to hello.jennifer.trace@gmail.com, I will send you some printable mazes for free.

My name is Jennifer Trace and I hope you enjoyed solving these mazes. I sure enjoyed creating them. If you have any suggestions about how to improve this book, changes to make or how to make it more useful, please let me know.

If you liked this book, would you be so kind and leave me a review on Amazon.

Thank you very much!
Jennifer Trace

Congratulations
Maze Super Star:

THE BEST!

Date:_____          Signed:_____

# SOLUTION

<sup>1</sup> PLAYTIME

<sup>2</sup> HI TURTLE

<sup>3</sup> LOST SHEEP

<sup>4</sup> BIKING

<sup>5</sup> PLAYGROUND

<sup>6</sup> FIREMAN

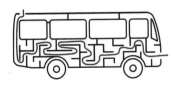

<sup>7</sup> THE BUS

<sup>8</sup> MR. TURTLE

<sup>9</sup> SANTA CLAUS

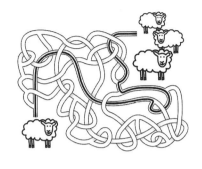

# SOLUTION

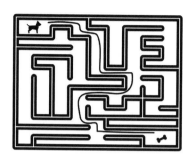

<sup>10</sup> HUNGRY DOG

<sup>11</sup> STRAWBERRY

<sup>12</sup> HOT AIR BALLOON

<sup>13</sup> PIG

<sup>14</sup> UMBRELLA

<sup>15</sup> HAPPY BIRTHDAY

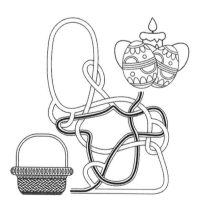

<sup>16</sup> EASTER

<sup>17</sup> PASTA

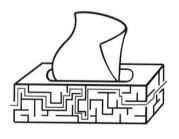

<sup>18</sup> TISSUE BOX

# SOLUTION

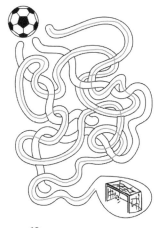

¹⁹ GOAL!

²⁰ ELEPHANT

²¹ GOING HOME

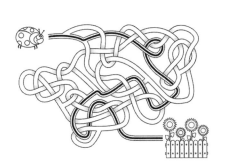

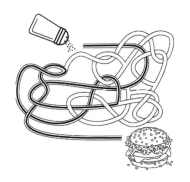

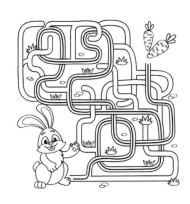

²² LADYBUG

²³ MORE SALT

²⁴ RABBIT

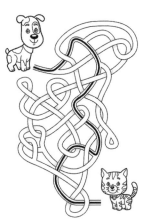

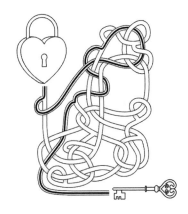

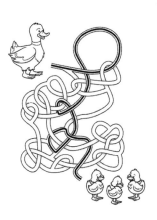

²⁵ FRIENDS

²⁶ UNLOCK

²⁷ TO MOMMY

# SOLUTION

 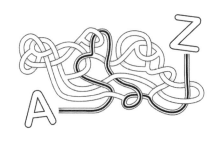 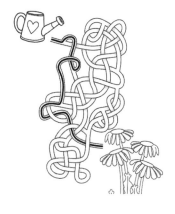

<sup>28</sup> LOST AND FOUND  <sup>29</sup> ALPHABET  <sup>30</sup> WATER THE FLOWER

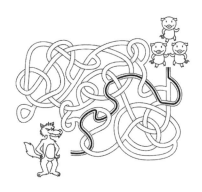  

<sup>31</sup> THREE LITTLE PIGS  <sup>32</sup> BASKETBALL  <sup>33</sup> HUNGRY GOLDILOCKS

<sup>34</sup> SAFARI  <sup>35</sup> OWL  <sup>36</sup> CATERPILLAR

# SOLUTION

<sup>38</sup> AVOCADO

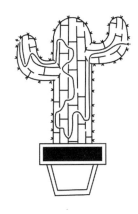

<sup>39</sup> CACTUS

<sup>40</sup> MERMAID

<sup>41</sup> BEE

<sup>42</sup> HELLO SNOWMAN

<sup>43</sup> THE CANDY CANE

<sup>44</sup> MR. WHALE

<sup>45</sup> THE MOON

<sup>46</sup> HAPPY DOG

# SOLUTION

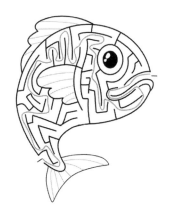

<sup>47</sup> UNDER THE WATER

<sup>48</sup> HI SNAIL

<sup>49</sup> ANGEL

<sup>50</sup> ROCKET SHIP

<sup>51</sup> FRUITS

<sup>52</sup> TRUCK

<sup>53</sup> CROCODILE

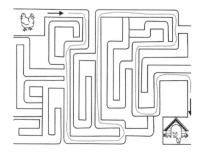

<sup>54</sup> LOST CHICKEN

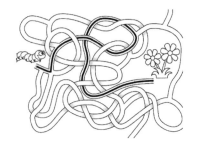

<sup>55</sup> CATERPILLAR

# SOLUTION

<sup>56</sup> GROCERY SHOPPING

<sup>57</sup> SNOWMAN

<sup>58</sup> DOCTOR

<sup>59</sup> APPLE TREE

<sup>60</sup> BUSINESS

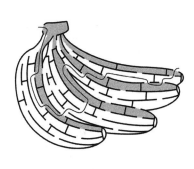

<sup>61</sup> BIG BANANA

<sup>62</sup> BUS TRIP

<sup>63</sup> FLY HOME

<sup>64</sup> GUITAR

# SOLUTION

65 FIRETRUCK

66 LOOKING FOR MAMMA

67 MUFFIN MAN

68 CHRISTMAS

70 DAILY CHORES

71 CHRISTMAS TREE

 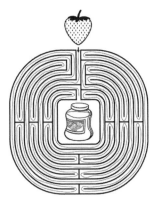 

72 SHELTER

73 STRAWBERRY JAM

74 WEEKEND BREAKFAST

# SOLUTION

75 HAPPY COW

76 DINING TABLE

77 BIRDS

78 COMING HOME

79 HALLOWEEN

80 MS. GIRAFFE

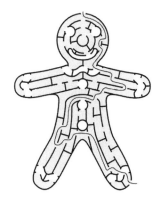

81 GINGERBREAD MAN

82 SEAHORSE

83 RIDING

# SOLUTION

84 PINEAPPLE

85 IN SPACE

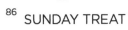

86 SUNDAY TREAT

87 EASTER EGG

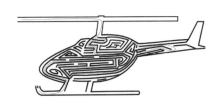

88 HELICOPTER

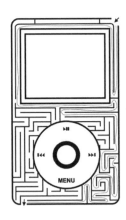

89 MP3 PLAYER

90 RAIN BOOTS

91 SPIDER WEB

92 MR. CRAB

# SOLUTION

93  TIGER

94  WAY HOME

95  BUTTERFLY

96  BALL

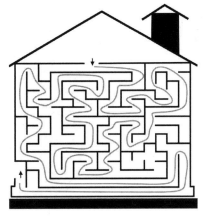

97  HOUSE

98  THANKSGIVING

99  TEDDY BEAR

100  FLOWER

101  TROPHY

# SOLUTION

102 BALLOONS

103 TUCAN